Best of luck, Debbie!!
Mary P.

To Love & To Cherish

To Love & To Cherish

by
DAVID E. WEBSTER
illustrated by Marvin Besunder

Published by The C. R. Gibson Company
Norwalk, Connecticut

*This book is dedicated
to the many successful
marriages about which
so little is heard or written.*

Copyright MCMLXVIII by
The C. R. Gibson Company, Norwalk, Connecticut
Printed in U.S.A.
Library of Congress Catalog Card Number: 67-29308

Introduction...

*Sometimes the simplest expressions provoke
the deepest thought. Those thoughts which spring
from heartfelt experience often mean more
than lengthy manuals of advice. No special artistry
or acute insight is claimed for the reflections
brought together in this book.
Yet, it is the hope of the author that some of these
observations on marriage will add
an extra degree of warmth, understanding
and thoughtful
consideration to more marriages.*

Togetherness...

*On board the sea of life
the principle of Noah's ark is best...
two by two.*

*Man is the head,
woman the heart
of a marriage.*

*Speak often of your love
to prove it is constant and undying...
the tide caresses the sands
twice each day
to whisper its song of eternity.*

Togetherness...

*Now and then gaze
at the face of your sleeping mate...
you will understand
how lucky you have been.*

*Sit together sometimes
in the darkness...
the past regroups joyously
and the future smiles.*

*Marriage needs three,
not just two...
remember God.*

*A willing ear can help
to banish trivial anxieties
that gnaw away at happiness.*

Togetherness...

*A marriage partner
is someone
to love with, laugh with, weep with,
work with, pray with, dream with
and live with.*

*Time spent together
is never wasted.*

*Happy times
shared in marriage
go on forever
as two shadows side by side
lengthen in the twilight of life.*

*One should give more to a marriage
than he takes from it.*

Togetherness...

*There is no time limit
on honeymoons.*

*Courtship is when a man
pursues a woman...
marriage is when she catches him...
and he's happy about it.*

*Nature and time are the authors of change
in a marriage...
but the partners
decide the eventual outcome.*

*Do not spend time
searching for happiness
within yourself.*

Togetherness...

*Marriage for love
is a noble undertaking.*

*Even the smallest things
your mate does for you
should never be taken for granted.*

*A successful marriage calls for
two career diplomats.*

*In courtship you look over appealing attributes...
in marriage you overlook minor faults.*

*Create memories you will be able to enjoy
again and again.*

Marriage is a reciprocal agreement.

Love, Especially Married Love...

*The song of love
has endless variations.*

*Real love is total . . .
it cannot be scheduled
or regulated.*

*Love can be given to all . . .
but married love is reserved for two.*

*Married love,
because of its difficulties,
is the most rewarding.*

Love, Especially Married Love...

Love is to do for ...
not to look for.

Love should be the cause ...
not the effect.

Love should be active
rather than passive.

Married love requires sacrifice.

Married lovers stay young forever.

Marriage is a diamond
of which love is the sparkle.

True love, far from being blind,
offers keen insight
into that which is hidden from others.

Love, Especially Married Love...

Love is sharing.

*True love is like a gentle wind ...
it cannot be seen,
but it refreshes and comforts.*

True love is God's creation.

*Love is the prized possession
of the emotionally wealthy.*

*The truest love is tempered
by the greatest adversity ...
fear nothing.*

*True love comes only once
in each person's lifetime ...
but if you cherish it,
that once is enough.*

Sign Posts Along The Way...

To believe
that there is more
than one ideal spouse for you
is an old wives' tale...
when you are married.

False pride has no place in marriage.

Marriage is not a spectator sport.

Respect your partner...
but not above the marriage.

The marriage vows
are the only restrictions
in a good marriage.

Sign Posts Along The Way...

*Expect ups and downs in your marriage...
a symphony could never be played
with only one note.*

Boredom is the sullen thief of happiness.

*Boredom is grounds only for adjustment...
not infidelity.*

Analysis that probes too deeply may destroy.

An unhappy marriage bed has many lumps.

Selfishness loosens the tie that binds.

*Hair of silver replacing gold
is never a reason
for love to grow cold.*

Sign Posts Along The Way...

Infidelity of mind can be longer lasting than infidelity of body.

Courtship shouldn't end once the marriage vows are taken.

Avoid intentional hurt.

Do not pressure each other.

Be a leader ... not a boss.

Reciprocate ... do not retaliate.

Marriage has no impossibilities.

Marriage is not to be submitted to ... it is to be attained.

The coldness of vengeful anger dampens the brightest flame.

Detours...

*The most difficult years of marriage
are the middle years...
the bloom is off
and the roots
may not have fully taken hold.*

*To withhold love
in the fear of being hurt
is to deprive marriage
of its essential ingredient.*

*Pity weakens love...
sympathy strengthens it.*

Detours...

*A critical word in public...
is a private wound
that may never heal.*

*Pains of marriage
can lead ultimately
to joyous pleasures.*

*Never say good night in anger...
love must end the day.*

*If you lay down the law...
be prepared for amendments.*

*Let your mate be...
you cannot change someone else
any more than you can change yourself.*

Detours...

*One who profanes the marriage union
is guilty of monumental corruption.*

*The surgery
necessary to save a worthwhile marriage
is often most painful...
but pain can be forgotten
by a healthy mind.*

*In love's garden,
infatuation is a night-blooming flower...
true devotion is a perennial.*

*A good marriage
will make you happy...
a troublesome one
will make you a philosopher.*

Steps To Married Bliss...

*Marriage is like two people
adrift on a life raft...
there is no room for discord
and close teamwork is necessary
to survive.*

*None of us is perfect...dwell on
your partner's
good points.*

*If there is
anything
better than
to be loved...
it is loving.*

*If no one loves you,
it's hard to prove you're alive.*

Steps To Married Bliss...

*Make the first step...
the second will follow.*

*A cruel word cannot be retracted...
but it can be forgiven.*

*Humor is the umbrella
which protects the marriage
on stormy days.*

*Praise your mate...
you'll be repaid once the shock is over.*

*A sincere kiss or a kind word
given in time of anger
often reduces or eliminates the anger.*

*People who play with marriages
are like children who play with matches.*

Steps To Married Bliss...

*Appreciate your partner's differences...
trying to change them will only
cause resentment and reduce the
breadth of your marriage.*

*The shortest distance between two points —
or two people — is a straight line...
strive for simplicity.*

*Better to clear the track
of small obstacles
than to derail the train.*

*Strength and stubbornness
should be used
only to achieve worthwhile goals.*

*It is easier to destroy than to build...
but look at the results.*

Steps To Married Bliss...

*Sometimes it is better
for strong emotion to be expressed ...
rather than repressed.*

*Know well your values ...
those that have lasted are best.*

*To run a race without knowing the goal
not only wastes your time and talents
but hampers those running with you.*

*Assume virtues are in each of you ...
with love they will be.*

*Respect your mate's mysteries ...
they enhance desire.*

You receive when you give.

Steps To Married Bliss...

*Marriage is not a contest . . .
sometimes to win is to lose.*

*A person who marches through life alone
is like a child making friends with his mirror.*

*Marriages are symbolized
by rings on fingers . . .
not rings through noses.*

*One does not leave a sick child
to suffer alone . . . nor a distraught mate.*

*Inflicting hurt is like throwing a boomerang . . .
it often returns harder than it is thrown.*

*A good marriage partner
is comparable to a good athlete . . .
he gives most when the going is toughest.*

Little Extras...

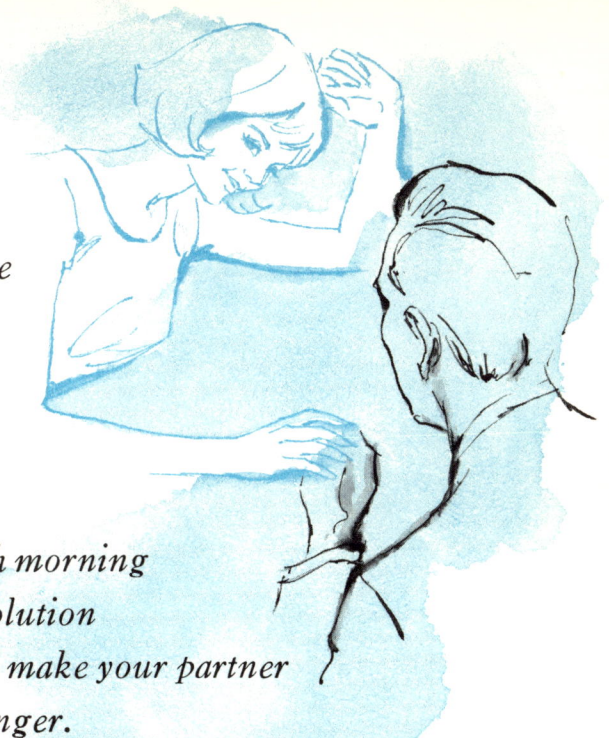

*Whisper
words of love
when lights
are low...
or anytime.*

*Start off each morning
with the resolution
that you will make your partner
one day younger.*

Praise your partner in the morning.

*Surprise your partner
with a love letter once in a while...
your words of love will be there
when you are not present.*

Little Extras...

Kisses are reminders
of a continuing love.

Words that praise
are etched forever on the loving heart.

A crumb is more important
to a starving man
than a loaf of bread
to a man who has just feasted.

No marital problem is so important
that it cannot wait
until tomorrow noon.

A mountain
can sometimes be gained
by graciously giving up
a grain of sand.

Little Extras...

*There is never enough time
to say what is in your heart.
The ticking of the clock
is the lover's enemy...
Say it now!*

*Repair the tiny flaws
with words of warmth.*

Little favors bring big returns.

*Nighttime is for marital joy...
not marital problems.*

*Words of praise
are always appreciated gifts.*

*Gaze often at your wedding photos...
relive the wonderment and joy.*

Marriage, Your Most Precious Possession...

*Many are the joys
encompassed in the tiny circle
of the wedding band.*

*We are all born for marriage...
it is our most precious heritage.*

*Despite the cynics,
romantic dreams can become joyful reality.*

*A marriage
should heighten
romantic dreams...
not shatter them.*

*Marriages leave
a legacy of love...
a hope for the future.*

*Marriage, Your Most
Precious Possession...*

Try tenderness.

Think love.

*Your mate
should be your last romantic date ...
and should be treated
as your first romantic date.*

Marriage is a point of honor.

Marriage is a full-time job.

*Remember, you married for better or worse ...
not for more or less.*

*Marriage, Your Most
Precious Possession...*

You are just born
when you say "I do."

" 'Till death us do part"
is the most meaningful phrase
you will ever utter.

 Each succeeding wedding anniversary
is the best.

Matrimony provides the key
to another's very soul...
guard it with your life.

Marriages are made in heaven...
pay homage to their birthplace.

Marriage, Your Most Precious Possession...

*Marriage is composed
of happiness, heartbreak, ecstacy and despair.
The blending of the ingredients
depends on the persons involved.*

*Your marriage houses tomorrow's generation...
give it a good home.*

Rejoice in your partner's graces.

*Nurture your marriage carefully
and watch it grow old gracefully.*

*If you must look back,
remember the good times ... not the bad.*

*Marriage, Your Most
Precious Possession...*

The many good apples
in the marriage bushel should not be soured
by the few bad ones...
the bad should be thrown out and forgotten.

A golden wedding band
never tarnishes or dulls...
neither should the marriage
it symbolizes.

Marriage for love
is a noble undertaking.

A marriage that flowers and blooms
is a private Garden of Eden.